Time For Healing
Reclaiming Life After Trauma

8/09

for Jackie

Complete Healing is Always possible!

Amy Maric

Time For Healing
Reclaiming Life After Trauma

Amy Groger Martin

 Healing Therapies Publishing
Niantic, Connecticut 06357

©2008 Amy Groger Martin. All rights reserved.

The entire content of this book is protected by copyright. No part of this book may be reproduced, republished, uploaded, transmitted or distributed in any manner without the written permission of the publisher.

Illustrations Copyright 2008 by Trish Morales
Design by Trish Morales
www.trishmoralesart.com
Edited by Karen C.L. Anderson
www.kclanderson.com

ISBN 978-0-9801202-4-0
ISBN 0-9801202-4-1

Disclaimer: This book is not intended as a substitute for professional counseling. If you are dealing with post traumatic stress, the services of a competent professional should be sought.

Names and identifying characteristics of people have been changed to protect the privacy of the individuals.

Healing Therapies Publishing
PO Box 347
Niantic, Connecticut 06357
www.healingtherapiespublishing.com

Printed in the United States of America

This book is dedicated to anyone who has experienced trauma and never believed they could completely heal, and for those helpers who reach deeply into themselves to assist victims in reclaiming their lives.

Time For Healing

Warning

In addition to descriptions of the healing process used, this story includes scenes of intense sexual violence and deviant behavior, which may be disturbing to readers.

This book may be particularly beneficial if you or someone you care about has experienced such deep trauma, that the thought of complete healing seems impossible.

Contents

Foreword XIII

Introduction XV

Part I

The Telling. 21

Hope's Story 25

The Questions 29

Imagining the Pain 35

Finding the Way. 39

Stepping Out Momentarily 47

A Trip Back In Time 51

Finding Out the Truth 53

Healing Is Possible 59

Part II

Hope's words: 65

Time For Healing

Tell It All 67

Keeper of the Darkness 73

Rescuing the Protector 81

Blood on a Cold Basement Floor 91

Heart vs. Head 97

Desert Girl 101

The Cement Block 107

Barbed Wire 111

The Swamp Monster 115

Healing the Tortured One 119

Dreams of Pain 127

The Brick Wall 131

Alone 135

Shadows and Light 139

Contents

Tammy 143

Resolution 147

Unresolved Connections 151

The Letter 155

Then vs. Now 161

Epilogue 165

PTSD Information and Resources 169

About the Author 175

Foreword

I have learned that when we choose to hide something, whether consciously or not, it has the potential to take on a life of its own. The unconscious impact of the act of concealment is now being more fully understood, as Post-Traumatic Stress Disorder (PTSD) is being studied in greater depth. Socking away traumatic experiences in the locked file cabinets of the consciousness requires ever-vigilant monitoring and demands greater amounts of energy as time passes. One who conceals events of the past may even "forget about it" for a time, but eventually, something comes up that triggers the memory. At that point more and more attention must be given to keeping the secret, with all its accompanying guilt and feelings of worthlessness, all the while denying its impact. It is only when one realizes that secrets buried alive never completely die, and is compelled to bring the truth into light, that those things hidden, finally lose their power.

I have had the opportunity to be a witness to the intense effects of Post-Traumatic Stress Disorder and have seen its debilitating impact and subsequent long-term degradation. The fact that there is hope for people who have experienced horrific trauma is amazing in itself. The use of imagery in healing is demonstrated in this dramatic story of transformation, as one woman, brave enough to unlock those filled-to-capacity file drawers, faces her demons and finally finds freedom.

This is a message of hope to anyone who feels hopeless, a promise of light to those still hiding in darkness. As you desire healing so it shall be. May you be blessed with a friend, a therapist or a family member who will love you and listen with a non-judgmental heart so that all things once hidden can be revealed and no longer have any power over you. Whatever you may have experienced, it is possible to heal. Let this story bring hope into your heart, to know there is a promise of relief, whether you believe it or not, and that you can be strengthened by this hope. May your burdens be lightened, your pain be eased and your wholeness be reclaimed

Please note that the names and places in this story have been changed. Even so, if any reader happens to recognize this unbelievable chain of events, we ask that no contact be attempted.

Amy Groger Martin APRN, BC, RhD
Board Certified Nurse Practitioner
Doctor of RoHun™ Transpersonal Psychotherapy

Introduction

On a frigid winter morning in December of 2004, a 48-year-old woman, known as "Roxie" was scheduled to be put to death by lethal injection in a high-security prison in the western United States when a last-minute stay of execution was handed down by the Governor. The prison reported the inmate became agitated and angered by the decision, and at the exact time she was to be executed, was found dead, hanging by her jumpsuit from the top bar of her cell gate. In this way, Roxie's 30-year reign of unfathomable violence finally came to an end.

In another part of the country, Roxie's death was the culminating event in a three-year process of uncovering and discovering, of facing truths and bearing witness to those truths, for my friend Hope. Hope never thought she'd be able to tell her story, a story she had neatly and safely tucked away in the secret vaults of her heart.

Deep down inside, however, Hope must have known that one day she would feel safe enough to tell someone about the horrific events that occurred in 1979 when she was an 18-year-old Freshman in college, an age when other girls are busy discovering themselves, expressing their independence and beginning to blossom into the women they would become.

It would be 25 years later that Hope would take down the walls she had so carefully constructed to keep her safe, sustaining her emotional isolation, and reveal her past; a past she thought would expose her as a monster and a misfit. She chose me to hear it and believed that simply telling the story would end it. Neither of us would have imagined the series of events that "the telling" would trigger, calling into action law enforcement and the judicial system in two states, giving six women a chance to exhale, and bringing the seventh to her death.

My intention is not to sensationalize a story of violence, shame or abuse, but to inspire those who can not imagine recovering from a trauma so deeply intense, that it took their soul.

My hope is that by telling this story, something good will come of it. The process of revealing and healing has allowed my friend Hope to blossom into a person of great compassion, one whose strength of spirit and depth of love is inspiring. She faced her fiercest demons, the memory of her own pain, and the knowledge of her potential to cause pain. It was through the power of

Time For Healing

her own determination and the assistance of imagery, along with raw self honesty, that she was finally able to forgive herself and begin to truly heal.

Part I

Telling her story was only the first step in a long and arduous journey, and her life as she knew it would never be the same.

Chapter 1
The Telling

Those who have hidden a part of themselves feel there is no choice but to keep their secrets. It's safer that way. They go through their lives locked up tight and seemingly secure, their friends and family having no idea of the darkness they hide, thinking they're just fine. If the opportunity arises and safe harbor is offered, they may consider telling their stories. Being able to lay it all down relieves them of the great burden so long carried and brings the possibility of healing.

How does such a person choose to set down his or her burden? Where, when and with whom? I am a Nurse Practitioner, therapist and a caring friend. For Hope, it was the confluence of the right time, person and place that provided her with the seedling of thought that sharing her history could become a reality. Telling her story was only the first step in a long and arduous journey, and her life as she knew it would never be the same.

It was a cool autumn evening when Hope finally asked me if it would be okay for her to share her account of what happened to her in college. I knew it would be a heavy story, as I had been told the superficial facts. I attempted to prepare myself, balancing the compassion of a friend with the neutral non-judgment of a therapist. We went to a quiet lake and sat in my car, looking at the reflection of the lights rippling in the water. She handed me a two-page typewritten missive. It was a bulletized list of the atrocities she had experienced. No emotion, just the facts. She sat in frozen stillness as I

The Telling

read through it, once, then again and then a third time so I could really take it in. I was filled with shock, horror, deep sadness, overwhelming anger and nausea. The last two words on the paper were, "Any questions?"

Powerful and severe emotional damage, indiscernible to an onlooker, was just beginning.

Chapter 2
Hope's Story

I asked Hope to go into more detail. She told me it started when she entered college as a freshman with a basketball scholarship and a bright future. Life was good and excitement was high. Goodbye family, hello

Time For Healing

new world. She was strong, idealistic, confident and talented...a true leader.

Before school started she participated in a campus basketball clinic where she caught the eye of Roxie, the Captain of the women's team. Roxie was dynamic and charismatic, and was quite capable of using these qualities to manipulate and control all those around her. She seemed to have an unusual power over everyone she met, including her team members, the coaches and staff. It didn't take long for Roxie and her gang to target Hope. They followed, stalked, coerced and then threatened Hope into joining their "girls club," trying to convince her that she was gay, telling her that she would be happiest only if she joined them.

"No thanks," she said innocently, "I'm not interested." She felt that they could live their lives in whatever way they pleased, but she would make her own choices. They would not take no for an answer.

Roxie and her six devoted followers steadily and systematically increased pressure on Hope to join. Then the violence began. She was chased, captured and taken to a secluded part of campus where she was tortured, beaten, raped and left for dead. She somehow found herself in an Emergency Room, requiring immediate surgery, and was left with irreparable injuries that would make it impossible for her to carry children. Powerful and severe emotional damage, indiscernible to an onlooker, was just beginning.

When she reported the assault to the police, the gang gave alibis for each other and with Roxie's powerful influence and manipulative personality, the group was out of jail within two hours. Their power was widespread and intense.

As all abusers will threaten their victims, so it was in this case. "This is what will happen if you ever report us again." Wanting to impress upon Hope her anger at being reported, and her capacity for future violence, Roxie and her gang abducted another freshman named Tammy, a friend of Hope's from her hometown. Tammy was subjected to the same violent brutality while Hope was tied to a tree, rendering her helpless, and forced to watch, "This will happen to every member of your family if you ever report us again."

So she didn't.

She would…scrub herself in the shower with the hottest water she could stand.

Chapter 3
The Questions

Now, another person might have left school right away and pursued other avenues of the law, but this 18-year-old girl made some pretty heavy decisions after this series of events. Hope decided that it was her responsibility to protect herself, her family and friends and to deal with this violence completely on her own. Was it because of the way she was brought up? Because she was taught to finish what she started? Was it her basic personality? Was it the threats, that even if she left school, her family would not be safe?

The brutal attacks, which included torture, stabbings, strangling, and sexual assault with weapons, as well as verbal degradation, continued through this first and only semester of school she would attend. The continued violence forced Hope into the most primal aspect of her personality: survival. Like a hunted animal they pursued her. She would return to her dormitory room bruised and bloodied, where she would scrub herself in the shower with the hottest water she could stand and watch her blood flow down the drain. No matter how hard she tried, she was never able to achieve the cleansing she so desperately needed.

I had so many questions:
How were you able to still attend classes?
How could your roommates ignore both your physical and emotional distress?
Why did you continue to deny there was anything wrong each time your parents called, and why did they believe you?

The Questions

How could NO ONE know you needed help?
Why didn't anyone protect you?
Why didn't you protect yourself?

It all sounded unbelievable to me, but in Hope's mind staying and fighting seemed to be her only option. She believed what they had told her: "If you leave, we'll find you…you're the only one who has ever said no… we'll break you if it's the last thing we do."

There is wildness in all of us that surfaces when we are pushed to the limit of our physical and mental pain. I think we've all asked ourselves if we could take a life if it was "us or them," or if our loved ones were being threatened. Hope actually had the chance to kill Roxie, but in the split second before she might have acted, Hope felt a gentle hand on her shoulder; the memory of a grandmother she had never met, stopping her from doing something for which she would never have been able to forgive herself.

After telling me her story she left the car and began wretching. After hearing her story, I was beyond shocked.

The next day we continued. I had more questions, curious about the details so blatantly ignored. So I began to ask her questions:

Time For Healing

How did you make these decisions?
What ever happened to Tammy?
Where are Roxie and the other women now?
How did you survive?
Why wasn't the law involved?
Why weren't they stopped?
How does Roxie still find your unlisted phone numbers and continue to threaten you, even though it's been more than 20 years?
Now what? How in the world can I help you?

She didn't have many answers. She didn't know what became of Tammy, only that she took her to the hospital, fabricated a story to the police and three days later found her wandering the campus in nothing but her underwear. Tammy left school and never returned.

She did know that Roxie and her group continued their reign of violence, even after Hope left college. They would find her, reminding her of their threats, reciting names, addresses and schedules of her family members. Their attacks continued on and off for years. They were absolutely psychopathologic, without any remorse or visible conscience.

These questions and answers were actually the beginning of how I helped Hope. Helping began the day after the telling, when I sat across from my friend and cried for her suffering. How could I NOT cry after hearing such an accounting of pain, shame, abuse and torture?

I will never know why my tears touched her heart at that moment, but it was that salty river that opened her heart and allowed her to feel compassion, for the very first time, for herself. It was the beginning of an energetic and emotional process, not simply a mental one, which ended up taking two years.

"No one has ever cried for me," she said.
Well, it's about time.

I want to shrink into a corner and disappear, never to be seen again.

Chapter 4
Imagining the Pain

I sat one morning and tried to understand and imagine what Hope went through. I believed it was necessary for me in order to help her. It was physically painful for me to put myself in her place, to understand what she must have felt, to feel the enormity of the impact of these life altering events.

In my mind I tried to touch the feeling of being a victim, of going to a place that no one ever wants to go.

I see, feel, taste and smell the horrific, sadistic, insane acts of violence; the sweat, blood, salt and slime; the frustration that swells up in the gut, the powerlessness, nausea and bile that never quite settles. I feel the horror of becoming a thing, a non-human; of being seen as an object without feelings, without a heart or soul, but something to be used; the inability to change the situation; and now, the inability to forget. Forgetting would be a gift and with it then forgiveness might be possible, but not now.

My mind sees and understands but my intestines wail with confusion and injustice. The assaults are not only on the body, but on the mind and heart, as well. History and potential and future are forever changed.

The grief is overwhelming and there is no safety zone. How can this be set aside? How can there be resolution? How can there be joy again? People say they come to stop asking why, but I'm not there. WHY? For what purpose was this experience, this pain and grief? But then I see I'm not ready for an answer.

Imagining the Pain

I want to shrink into a corner and disappear, never to be seen again. How could anyone allow themselves to be so vulnerable? Was it just innocent trust, the inconceivability of true evil? And even after it was seen, it still was not believed

My stomach tightens when I watch the scenes; if it were a movie, I'd close my eyes or leave the theatre. It pulls my guts out, leaving emptiness. Then the next scene fills the emptiness with the fire of rage and violence, the need to retaliate, to claim some sense of power, to take back some of what was stolen. The light was taken away – the hope of light, of God, of love. Only darkness remained, only shadows and deception and lies and plans to destroy. Life changed, hope died, plans forever altered as this rage continued to fester. The heart slowly but surely closed down, shut the doors, locked up tight and a wall of impenetrability was created. No one, no thing would ever be allowed close because it was vulnerability, weakness and passiveness that caused this. These will never be allowed. NEVER. Alone, isolated, rock like…hard, closed, fists clenched, eyes squeezed shut…never open, never let anyone affect this life…NO!

I felt limited in my ability to empathize, but I reached into my own pain in hopes of seeing what Hope needed

Time For Healing

to heal. What was most difficult for me to understand was her cold detachment, her emotional anesthesia. Where were the tears? Where was the rage? But she showed nothing, not one shred of emotion. I understood intellectually that she was unable to let herself feel. She feared the emotions would drown her, deeming her incapable of continuing life as she knew it.

I had more questions:
Can you ever truly forgive for having had your life taken away?
How will you find peace and resolve?
What steps are needed to come to that place?
Where do we go from here?

I felt a prayer bubbling up within me: Heal our hearts, help us love ... wholeheartedly.

Chapter 5
Finding the Way

I am trained in RoHun™ Therapy, a spiritually based psychotherapeutic tool that opens the way for transformation and change. It uses set processes to uncover and bring to light those events in one's life that have caused continued pain and isolation. This therapy has the capacity to go right under the defenses of the ego, revealing the shadows of the unconscious mind, faulty thoughts and negative emotional reactions, freeing a person to reclaim his or her wholeness.

RoHun™ Therapists are trained to intuitively see what their clients are seeing, sensing and feeling, in order to assist in identifying and releasing unhealthy patterns. This is the kind of therapy that actually helps someone find their emotional center of gravity, and release their habitual reactions which have become ingrained over time.

Carl Jung talked about "reactive selves:" the judging self, the helpless self, the frightened self, the unworthy self, and many others, all of which are part of the personality. RoHun™ therapists support the understanding of how these various reactive selves block, restrict, limit and continually sabotage their clients; they also address how these "selves" may be serving them in some unhealthy way. It is the individual's conscious choice to release these reactive selves, or not. By understanding choices made in the past and evaluating the effects of these choices on the present, the individual can move toward forgiveness and release both the negative thoughts and these instant emotional reactions that hinder progress.

Finding the Way

The greatest gift of RoHun™, in my experience, is seeing people acknowledge their own wisdom and become cognizant of their 'higher self' and then incorporate that strength and enlightenment in their self understanding.

I knew we would use RoHun™ Therapy as part of Hope's healing, but also blend in some gentle imagery and deep progressive relaxation, as the effects of her experience were so severe. We would start slowly, letting any images she had come into focus and then begin our exploration them. For example, if she were to bring up the picture of that "helpless self," the one who found herself repeatedly victimized, I could get her to look into the eyes of that person and imagine what she must have been feeling. We could find the dominant thought she had about herself at that moment and the decisions she made about life. At that point we would talk about how that sense of helplessness has impacted her life and how it has affected her over time.

I wanted Hope to see and understand the core of her emotional reactions and their impact on both her daily life and her relationships. When she saw that every emotion started with a thought, she could begin to capture those negative thoughts, become aware of their source and correct them. This then brought the possibility of freedom into her mind.

Time For Healing

I knew the RoHun™ method could help Hope, but we needed to take it slowly and I needed to follow her lead. I wanted her to feel her own sense of personal strength and to help her remember who she was, underneath all the pain. I knew she needed to forgive herself first and foremost, but I also knew that it would be a long time in coming. The answers would come when she was able to acknowledge weakness, admit powerlessness and forgive herself for every wrong choice.

As we came to this point, I felt her fatigue. I couldn't imagine being in her position, and even holding my own head up. I realized that she could have easily died, but no; she survived and continues to suffer the torment of memory.

But I also saw her need to rise above misery, to see with clarity and comprehension that all trials and tribulations are but a small moment in the course of eternity, and that all experience offers a depth of compassion that could not come otherwise. Rising above would help her see this from a more distant perspective and allow her to forgive as she learned long-sightedness.

I felt a prayer bubbling up within me: Heal our hearts, help us love...wholeheartedly.

Finding the Way

I followed my intuition and my gut, and with her approval, began digging and asking more questions. Each day we worked together, she was more willing to talk about the events. She spoke in images, as if what she physically experienced was something she saw in a picture. She would then describe where she was emotionally. It was easier for her to talk about emotions in the third person, as if she were looking at someone, not herself, in a picture. So instead of asking her to tell me what she was feeling, I asked her to imagine what the girl in the picture was feeling. We used these pictures to distance her from the events, but also to allow her to see it for what it was. She described a host of characters, all of whom represented her self, in different situations.

At times the work seemed insurmountable; the pain felt, was overwhelming. She needed help beyond what she and I could do together, and so we brought in the strength of her faith. Sometimes we need the support of a higher power, of someone or something stronger than ourselves, to face our demons. Some use God or Christ or Angels, and those who prefer something more generic, ask for help from "The One Who Cares." The One Who Cares has a power of love within that can heal anyone, help in any situation and bring courage and strength when needed. Because Hope was raised in a family believing in Christ, this image brought her great comfort and this was the mental picture we used during our healing processes.

And so together we found all the broken and fractured aspects of her psyche: the bloodied, naked girl lying bound on a cold, basement floor; the desert girl, standing isolated in a silent and colorless world; the girl standing watch at the mountain of emotions and experience, so no one would enter, and the dying and suffering girls hidden within that mountain. We found the girl who felt bound by a cement block, and the girl whose throat felt like it had been stuffed with barbed wire. Most difficult of all was discovering the character she called the swamp monster, the image Hope had of herself as the horrible abuser she believed she became when she retaliated against the gang who tried to destroy her.

Discovering each hidden girl took time, from a few hours, to many days, but she was eventually able to come to terms with every single event that happened to her and face what she had done in response. It also took every ounce of both her and my energy, strength, imagination and faith.

Even now, when I recall this time, I feel the waves of exhaustion – and of exhilaration – at the amazing changes that took place over the two years Hope and I worked together.

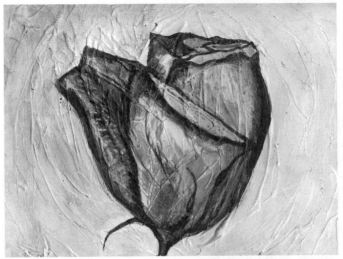

We would loosen her tightened fists with gentle persuasion, as one would open the petals of a rose.

Chapter 6
Stepping Out Momentarily

There were moments during this process that I found myself questioning my ability to help. At times, Hope would become quiet, with long delays in her responses. Her thinking was already quite slow and she might

Time For Healing

take five to 10 minutes to answer a simple question. She seemed to fall deeper into herself and I was only occasionally successful in bringing her back quickly. She exhibited all the symptoms of Post-Traumatic Stress Disorder, including intrusive thoughts and memories of the events where she would actually re-experience the trauma, persistent avoidance of emotions with numbing of her general responsiveness and increased arousal, difficulty sleeping, recurrent nightmares and a sense of hypervigilance with an exaggerated startle response.

She then began to have periods of dissociative states, during which time she would re-live the events as though experiencing them in real time. It was at these times that she became totally unresponsive. These states would last anywhere from a few minutes to a few hours. Her hands would tighten into fists, followed by a deeper tightening of her entire body. Her breathing would become shallow and she would groan in pain, her body reacting to past traumatic events. Her arms would take on the position of having her wrists bound. She would clench her hands so intensely that her palms would bleed.

She described these dissociative states as pure darkness, a freefalling loss of consciousness in which she was totally unaware of her surroundings. She simply fell into her past experience with all its gory detail.

By this time we were working with the assistance of others, including her husband, and the only thing we could do to retrieve her from this place was hold her and wait. We would loosen her tightened fists with gentle persuasion, as one would open the petals of a rose: with the gentle warmth of loving hands. It was her husband who urged her to consider treatment with psychiatric medications.

Although she was initially resistant, she agreed when she realized this would be a long and difficult process. An SSRI (Selective Serotonin Reuptake Inhibitor), indicated for the treatment of PTSD, started to work within the first few weeks of its use, allowing her to sleep and find a sense of inner balance once again.

She returned home speaking about a new sense of space within her, room for her family, for her friends and finally, for joy.

Chapter 7
A Trip Back In Time

After the telling and several months of therapy, Hope began doubting her memories. She felt the need to return to the campus where it all took place; she had to see for herself that it wasn't just in her imagination

Time For Healing

and that she hadn't made it all up. The campus was a highly charged place, one that would stimulate bile and dread every time she passed it on the highway.

She went alone, moving from place to place on and off campus, and allowed herself to remember. She was sick more than once and had to tell herself that while this was a place where evil happened, it was now over. Her only job was to see it clearly for what it was.

She returned home utterly exhausted, knowing without a doubt that all her memories were correct, and that other events had taken place as well, ones that she was just beginning to remember.

With this courageous act, going back with the intention of healing, Hope allowed herself to be emptied completely, to have the weight taken from her, the sadness and grief removed, the hatred and self loathing spilled out, right there on that campus. As she completed her journey she realized that she could suddenly see everything around her, the colors of the sky, and the beauty of the mountains, all there as they had always been. She returned home speaking about a new sense of space within her, room for her family, for her friends and finally, for joy.

They told her that it was her courage to say no, that gave them hope that they could be free.

Chapter 8
Finding Out the Truth

When she returned from her trip, Hope was ready for more answers. She wanted to find out what happened to Tammy. After many phone calls to former classmates she finally spoke to someone who said, "You

Time For Healing

mean you hadn't heard? Tammy committed suicide 15 years ago." The shock, dread and guilt were immediate. Of course she blamed herself; if Tammy hadn't known Hope, she'd be alive. Hope was compelled to speak with Tammy's family.

Tammy's mother shared the history of her mental illness, which was present before the assault, but worsened afterwards. It seemed that Tammy was never able to get her life together, and despite psychiatric intervention, her hopelessness prevailed, and she took her own life at the age of 28. Hope's regret deepened as she learned more details of what Tammy suffered through the years since college, and she decided that it was time; Roxie must be stopped.

She wrote a letter to the authorities of the prison where Roxie was being held on recent assault charges and did something she had never thought she would ever do. She told her story, naming Roxie and the other six women who had been involved. She gave dates and detailed the events. She implored the state to never release this woman, this sexual predator, from prison. She expressed her guilt over not reporting this sooner, but also explained what happened when she reported the first assault. She wrote about Tammy and her suicide, the "altercations," the rapes, the stabbings, the strangling, being set on fire, the destruction of personal property, and the emotional toll it played on her life. She also wrote about the long healing process she was currently undergoing.

When she mailed that letter she knew she finally did what she should have done years ago, and she hoped it wasn't too late.

She also learned that the six women who had been part of the assaults and torture had, over time, parted with Roxie and made lives for themselves. I cannot imagine how they lived with the guilt of what they had done, but some were married, some with children. Some of them had, over the years, attempted contact with Hope to ask for her forgiveness. They told her that it was her courage to say no that gave them hope that they could be free from Roxie; no one had ever said no to her. Although she never responded to them directly, over the years Hope realized that these women, as heinous as their crimes had been, were also victims, thinking they had no choice but to follow Roxie's lead. They had taken Hope to the hospital after that first assault, and for that Roxie brutally beat them, degraded them, and made them feel worthless in every way, except in their capacity as her minions.

The women were aware of Roxie's whereabouts and would let Hope know where she was, in an attempt to protect her from accidental contact. It was one of these women who told Hope that Roxie had become a school teacher, so she made a report to the Board of Education in that town, relaying information regarding Roxie's previous arrests and sexual predator status. Roxie was fired. And only a few years ago, while visiting family in her hometown, Roxie spotted Hope in a shopping mall, and 'sucker punched' her in the back, resulting in fractured ribs. Because there were witnesses who reported it, Roxie was arrested when police discovered she was carrying a concealed weapon.

After that, the last Hope heard was that Roxie was under permanent house arrest for more assaults, had a tracking device attached to her ankle and was on heavy psychiatric medication.

During the first year of our exploration together, the authorities contacted Hope and told her that Roxie had escaped house arrest; Hope was told to warn her family to lock their doors and alter their usual routes because they may be in danger. They finally understood Roxie's potential for violence. Hope's anxiety was off the charts as she followed the details of the investigation to locate Roxie.

Finding Out the Truth

And then Hope had a vision. As clearly as if seeing it happen, Hope saw Roxie's plan. This phenomenon is called a psychic connection and it often occurs between victims and their abusers. The reasons for it are complex and mainly survival-motivated, but it can serve in many ways. Hope knew that Roxie would try to contact one of the six women, and she knew which one it was, and that she would go to this woman's previous address, because Roxie didn't know she had moved.

Hope immediately called the police but had to convince the officer on duty that although she was across the country, she knew where this escaped convict was. "Have you ever just known with every fiber of your being? I just know," she quietly but assuredly told the police. He decided to believe her, set up a sting operation and captured Roxie the next day, exactly where Hope said she would be.

Somewhere along the path I forgot to express that I love my life, but I do, I really do.

Chapter 9
Healing Is Possible

Three years and two months after the telling, Roxie was dead. Because of Hope's letter and Roxie's recent escape, her information was flagged on the court's computer system and it linked her to DNA evidence in an ongoing investigation of the murders of two young women in a neighboring state. She was extradited to that state where she was convicted of those crimes and given the death penalty. Hope and I tried to obtain the details of Roxie's trial, but were told that the records had been sealed for 50 years. There were no details of the crime for which she was given the death sentence, there was no Internet information regarding her status as a female death row inmate, and no report of her suicide was made public. Hope only received official word of Roxie's death because she continued to inquire, but it was firmly suggested by the prison authorities that she ask no more questions.

It is done. It is finished, and Hope is a different person now. She has allowed herself to feel, to be tender hearted and emotional. She has allowed her heart to be exposed and to experience all of life, with every bit of its messiness, pain and sadness, but now she can also feel all the joy, love and light and abundance as well.

She recently wrote to me and said, "I have been thinking a lot about gratitude and how blessed my life is, how easy my life is. Gratitude for my soul, I think I could have lost it. I am grateful for my strength, for my gifts and talents. Somewhere along the path I forgot to express that I love my life, but I do, I really do."

Part II

After I was at peace and still, I asked her to sit by my side and I took her hand ... and told her the rest of what happened to me.

She listened in stillness, watching my face and I recounted my ... history. My friend did not move or utter a sound, but her face revealed the working of her heart, showing me horror, rage, sympathy, compassion.

*When I finished, she shook her head. "I see why you did not tell me this before" she said sadly. "I wish I had been able to help you bare this burden from the very first. But now that you entrust your past to my keeping, it is safe I know you need no oath from me or else you would not have told me. "Dear one" she said, putting my hand to her cheek, "I am so honored to be the vessel into which you pour this story of pain and strength ... now I know who you are and what life has cost you. I am in awe that I number you among my beloved.**

---

* Anita Diamont: The Red Tent, p.298

Part II

It is with Hope's complete approval that her part of the story is being shared. The following chapters are a taste of what she went through in her process of healing. The original letter she gave me in the car that day of the telling is included, although some of the details have been edited. There are journal entries of thoughts and feelings that she was urged to record, and images of the fractured parts of herself that so sorely needed healing.

I only can move through this moment by moment, day by day, having faith and hope that all will be well.

Chapter 10
Hope's words:

The decision to have this story put to print has not been an easy one; I agonized over it for many months. Just the thought of having anyone read it brought on turmoil in the deepest parts of me. It conjured up feelings of alarm and dread. Just know that this book that you hold in your hands had to be written, although my gut has screamed NO! My head would say, "You can't share this, bad things will happen," and my heart so newly opened and still very tender would whisper, "It will be okay, this needs to be." I have had no remarkable, earth shattering or enlightened answers; I only can move through this moment by moment, day by day, having faith and hope that all will be well, and that more good will come from this story in its sharing.

I have never told anyone before, but this explains a little of how far and deep my emotions run.

Chapter 11
Tell It All

October 2001
I begin by calling this a story, because I think that if I do, it may be easier. For the first time in my life, I will

reveal those things that I have kept hidden, locked and lost within my being.

I have always had a fierce allegiance to those that I love and care about. I am sure at times that I have taken this to a level that is detrimental to me. There are people in my life for whom I would sacrifice my own life, and I would do so with no hesitation. Yeah, I know it sounds very melodramatic and I guess that's why I have never told anyone before, but this explains a little of how far and deep my emotions run. In my heart I care so little about my own life in comparison to those that I love.

Okay so I guess I'm stalling. I cannot even begin to express how much I DO NOT want to do this! I want answers. I want to know why I need to expound in full detail this part of my past. I think I've done very well so far not letting it consume my life. I could have let it control me. It could have destroyed me. It has not been easy and I have had my moments. But they were only moments and over the years I have been able to recover quicker each time. Why do I have to do this now? Why now, when it takes so much mental effort to deal with the pain. I DO NOT WISH TO DO THIS! So I guess the question is why.

I am afraid that I will not be able to stay in control. Now when I say control, I only mean control of my own emotions. The sick feeling in my stomach, head and heart when I have talked even about a small portion of this is so overwhelming to me. My whole body goes into shock and I begin to physically shake. If my internal reaction to just the parts that I have already shared is this dramatic, I cannot even imagine what condition I would be in if I shared everything with someone. I can endure physical pain, but my own hand has never purposely inflicted the pain that I have endured. To tell everything would be like stabbing myself with a dull instrument over and over again. Why in the world would I want to do that to myself? I don't understand this. I don't even know how to prepare for this. I never thought I would have to do it. I have gone through the gamut of emotions: anger, trepidation, peace, and back to anger with the cycle continuing. Even as I write this, I know without doubt that I will do what I know I must do, so why can't I just move on? If I say it out loud does that make it real? I know it was real, I was there. Why must I see and watch it again? Why does someone else have to see it too? It's 3:00 a.m. I need to sleep.

I have considered writing this story down or maybe I could just make up a list: "Things that happened to

Time For Healing

Hope." Hmm, "happened" makes it sound like none of this was my fault. Well let's see if a list would work. I'll start with the items I have already shared a little:
Beaten (too many times to count)
Cut (a couple of times)
Drugged (once)
Followed everywhere I went
Personal property destroyed
Run off the road (vehicular chicken)
Made to watch as they beat and raped a former friend of mine from grade school
Spread rumors about me in my hometown
Given exact schedules of family and friends
Stripped and handcuffed to a bed (Don't know how many times)
Raped and sodomized

Then there was the verbal abuse while all this is going on that no one could ever love me now except for Roxie
Threatened to do all the above and more to my family and friends

I am not blameless in this, for I had a part, I had opportunities to decide my reactions and I did not choose well. I was filled with hate, anger and extreme panic to protect my family and friends. I know the capacity of evil in my heart; I know how it can dictate your every move in life and every thought and wish. It had such control over who I was becoming. Everyone has parts of them that they wish no one to see. My part is the ugliness, meanness and darkness that I have the capability of retaining. Yes you can say that we all have that capability, but I watched myself unleash these feelings and actually act upon them. My fear is that in letting this out I will lose control over that piece, and that it could somehow escape and become a part of me again.

I beat several women
I was responsible for some of them losing their jobs and homes
I caused permanent physical and mental damage to some of them
I had every intention of ending a life (not my own)
I became the great defender of all
If I failed, others would suffer and it would be my fault
I trusted no one
I no longer allowed myself to love or care for anyone new
I shut the world out
NO ONE was allowed into my heart

I have story after story of times that I took great pleasure in watching their pain. I could go into great detail of how my temper would instantaneously flash, and I would be left looking at the blood, the bone, and hearing their cries for help, and I…would just simply walk away. That's right! Walk away to fight yet another day! What kind of sub-human would do that? Look at what I had become! Some kind of underworld animal with no thought or care of the pain and suffering that it had caused. Taking such pleasure in torture that it couldn't wait until the next time and in so doing would make itself "available" bait to make it happen.

It seems so long ago and that it lasted for a lifetime when in reality the worst and most intense part lasted only a little over a year. The rest was spread out over almost 20 years.

I'm not sure this is what I was supposed to write but it's the only way that I could crack open the door.

Any questions?

She had a huge block in front of her — a block as huge as a mountain.

Chapter 12
Keeper of the Darkness

When I asked Hope what she was feeling in the week after she told me her story, she described the task as monumental. She would have to look honestly at how she was affected, and realized that she had a huge block in front of her – a block as huge as a mountain. I asked her to look at its detail and draw it. This is how we began our work, looking into these images, drawing them, describing them and eventually thoroughly exploring each one.

~

November 2001
In front of me is a huge mountain with an opening at its base. It is soft but unyielding and I cannot go inside. It scares me to look at it. There is no way around it. Without going inside, the only direction I can go is backwards. As I contemplate this situation I wonder what is inside and I feel terrified. I see a young woman standing at the entrance to this place. She looks innocent and pure, of slender build with long dark hair. Her skin is perfect and white. She looks at me with huge, sad eyes but does not speak to me.

At first, the mountain seemed green in color, but as I began to draw it on paper, I realized that the color had changed to black. The young woman let me look inside, and what I sensed was a swirl of emotions, every one that I had buried in order to survive. Within this huge structure I saw:

Anger
Fear
Hatred
Aloneness
Doubt
Claustrophobia
Pain
Frustration
Sorrow
Distrust
Despair
Grief
Agitation
Panic

What was I supposed to do with all these feelings? At first I thought that I would have to write about my experience with each and every one, so I could cope and deal with them, let them out to finally be done. Every time I tried to do this I would freeze, be unable to think, and simply couldn't proceed at all. I then realized that my list was not complete. It took me days to finish identifying every single emotion held inside of this mountain. These were the ones that were missing:

Embarrassment
Shame
Torment
Sadness

Time For Healing

Disgust
Detachment
Uncertainty
Loss
Confusion
Anxiety
Disappointment
Discouragement
Mourning
Desolation
Hopelessness
Disgrace
Isolation
Emptiness

I didn't want to go inside, but a thought occurred to me; I wondered if the young girl could go in. I asked her, and she nodded her head and then spoke to me. She said these feelings are all mine, but she keeps them safe for me. At that point, I named her The Keeper of the Darkness. She would enter into the darkness and I would be allowed to see everything through her eyes.

It was very claustrophobic and I had trouble breathing, but then I started to watch as the feelings I had written appeared like hanging placards, signs floating in the dense and dark air within the cave. The Keeper of the Darkness looked as if she was performing a ballet. I watched as she would reach her hands high up into the air and take hold of one of the emotions, then she would spin around in a circle and with the other hand reach into my past to take hold of one of my traumatic experiences, and then bring both hands together. She would then bring these to her heart and hold them there for a moment, as if she was matching the emotion to the event, and then she would re-live the experience along with the emotion.

That's when I began to be aware of the feelings of pain screaming through her body. Each time she would go through these motions I would see the emotion she would choose and then I would see the attack that I experienced. She was actually connecting the intense emotions with each horrific assault. She was allowing herself to experience the feelings that I had turned off and buried. She had kept this pain hidden and guarded for me, and had not known what it felt like until now, as she continued to arduously work through every one of my experiences. As I watched her and felt everything she was feeling my entire body began to go into spasm. I was re-living the entire series of traumatic events, only this time I was feeling it in my heart.

The Keeper noticed me outside the entrance, curled up tightly contracted, and came out of the darkness to kneel beside me. She touched my head and calmed me,

Time For Healing

telling me it was not time for this, and the spasms stopped. She came out because I was in distress and she did not want me to be alone. I had several sessions where the Keeper would continue to work at matching the emotions to another horrific memory. She would work until she was exhausted, or until the magnitude of emotions of re-living of the past caused her too much distress and she could no longer go on. She began experiencing difficulty and appeared to be losing strength and stamina. The sessions were very limited and it would not be very long before she would come out and fall into my arms. She needed extra strength so I started to think about and visualize all those that I loved and who loved me. I wanted her to feel and experience the comfort and support that comes from them; I thought about everyone in my life, friends, family and the power of The One Who Cares. I wanted her to feel all the love and support that was in my life, and she was amazed at the power it possessed. It was a huge help to her in the sessions to come. I was able to look at the picture that I had drawn of the black mountain and see the emotions I had written down. They were diminishing as I realized I could look at some of them and know that they had been looked at, felt and given a place to safely reside.

There were two that were still there and very strong and daunting: fear and anger. I asked the Keeper about them and why she had passed them by. Her answer was not surprising and yet the reality of her words seemed to jump out, bringing the deepest sense of dread and fear that I could ever remember. She said that she could not release them. These last remaining two were my responsibility, and at the appropriate time, I would be granted entrance into the mountain to claim them.

I had wondered where the water had come from and I saw it was the accumulation of thousands of silent tears.

Chapter 13
Rescuing the Protector

After some time, Hope felt ready to go inside this mountain of feelings and see what else she'd been hiding from herself. This experience was the true beginning of her long road to healing.

Time For Healing

~

The day has come to gather courage and ask to go into the mountain. I am reminded of the love and acceptance of The One Who Cares, the atonement and power of light that is available.

I am standing at the entrance to the mountain and the Keeper comes near. She asks if I am ready and I reply, "Yes." I invite The One Who Cares to come with me and he agrees. The Keeper says that she will escort us in so that we can get used to the uneven terrain, and to be careful because it is slippery. We enter. The deep darkness is palpable; this place is HUGE and seems to go on forever. I am guided to look around for an entryway to a deeper room; I am told to look upward and begin searching, until I finally see a ledge with a very small door, the size a mouse could fit through. I must climb to it. I begin my ascent, rocky and wet; it is extremely hard to keep my feet from sliding off the protruding rocks. I finally make my way to this ledge and I look, unbelieving at this small door. I know I must go through it but not sure how to proceed.

I know I must open the door. As I touch the tiny handle the door changes to a full size door and I am

Rescuing the Protector

allowed entry to the other side. Through this door is yet another huge room. It is dark, but I can see it is filled with hundreds of young women. Most of them turn to look at me. I am startled by their appearance in that they all look like me, but very unkempt and dirty; their skin appears to be translucent, their gazes fixed and blank. They see me, yet they do not. I walk through the midst of them. Some follow, but some ignore me.

I am drawn to one girl in particular and I am alarmed. She appears to be only about 14 years old and I am puzzled by her age, but it quickly becomes clear why she is there. I was 14 when I decided what I wanted to do with my life, where I would go to college, what I would be, who I would become. All that was taken away from me, every last shred, my hopes, my dreams and my goals all were destroyed. I needed to tell her that even though those things had been vanquished, other dreams and goals had been created and that all hope was not lost. She stayed close and followed me, and a gleam of hope was growing within her. I heard her thoughts: did she dare believe?

Another young woman caught my attention, she was down on her hands and knees and she would not look up. Her hair was stringy, matted and hanging in her face. Her skin was rotting; she had large infested sores all over her body, she was dying. No matter how hard I tried she would not look up at me. I lay down on my back and wormed my way beneath her head so that I could see her face and she could see mine. It was like looking into the eyes of the dead; I wanted to scream but all I could do was cry. I sat up and truly took in the sight of all these wasted and emaciated young women, now looking intently upon me, looking to me to take them away from this place they had been for so long.

I envisioned rays of light coming down from above and sensed shafts of light piercing the blackness. The young women began to lift their faces to the rays of light, drinking it in. They drank as travelers who had sojourned across a barren, desert wasteland. I watched as a most amazing thing began to take place. These young women began to heal, slowly becoming clean and healthy, their hair beginning to shine in the radiant shafts of light that filled the entire room. These young women had been waiting for me, waiting for me to release them and take them out of this place; they thought this day would never come.

I beckoned them to follow me and I wondered if I had everyone. I turned back to look, and realized they were not following me. They would not look at me but I knew without a doubt I did not have everyone, and knew they would not leave without every last person. I began to search, but could not see anyone else. Shining light in every possible corner, I finally found a fissure off to the side, and behind a jagged piece of rock, I saw a form standing, unmoving and silent. She was fully dressed in a suit of armor. This was The Warrior, the protector, always watching from the hidden parts of this place. With much coaxing she emerged. Her nerves were frayed and tight. With a cold stare she told me to leave. This was her place, these girls were her responsibility, and I had put them in danger because now someone could find them.

I asked her to come with us out of this place, that it was time to take off her armor, that she no longer needed to protect them. It was time for her to join them and be healed. She refused. I asked The One Who Cares to come and speak with her. The Warrior became agitated at his presence. He reached out to take her hand and she backed away from him. I suddenly realized that the place was filling with water, and she was walking out into it. As The One Who Cares would take one step closer, The Warrior would take one step backwards, keeping the distance between them equal at all times.

The One Who Cares asked me to take his hand then told me to reach for her with my other hand. I once again asked her to come and to join the others, but she again refused. She began to re-play every scenario, the recurrent violent confrontations and attacks, to prove that she was still needed to protect. I became weak and nauseated from watching yet again all those moments from my past. The One Who Cares interrupted and asked if he could come to her. He tried to make her understand that this part of her was no longer needed, that these girls were no longer in danger and that they were in a safe harbor within his ever-watchful care. He commended her on her steadfastness and loyalty, for certain it was she who guarded and protected them well. She had kept them safe from harm, but now it was time for all of them to leave this place forever. He told her that these girls would not leave without her and begged her to retire her stance and vigilance and take rest and solitude within his protection and care.

I asked them all to come into the water and surround The Warrior. I wanted them to thank her for what she had done and to thank her for her sacrifice in their behalf. She needed to feel their love and support. She needed to know that they wanted her to come with them. They slowly walked around her; step-by-step they came closer to her. They were behind her and The One Who Cares and I were in front of her, letting our feelings and thoughts be transmitted to her. We needed to give her the courage to

Rescuing the Protector

let the armor fall and let the watchman come home. She looked as though she was being torn apart, her desire and habit had been but one: To Protect.

She struggled with the fear that in the future she might be needed again, and what if she was not ready? What if she failed? She would never be able to live with that. The girls came even closer to her, reaching out and touching her, something that they had never been allowed to do in the past. She shivered and groaned at their touch. I reached for her and asked to help remove her armor, she simply said no, commenting that it was not that easy. Tears were forming in her eyes. This shift in her world was discomforting to her; all she had ever known was now changing. The One Who Cares came forward and in a soft but commanding voice, assured her that her abilities to protect would probably never be needed again, but in the rare case should a time arise, He Himself would help her shoulder her armor one more time. "Come with us," the girls who still surrounded her spoke in unison. She looked at all of them, felt their love and gratitude. She fell backwards into the water and was submerged. It was The One Who Cares who brought her out of the water, and her armor was gone. It was that simple.

I had wondered where the water had come from and I saw it was the accumulation of thousands of silent tears.

Time For Healing

That is what made the inside surface of the mountain slippery and what had created this huge body of water.

We began to exit this room. I was busy thinking how I was going to get all these girls down the wall to the other room. I stopped to look back; they had stopped and were looking at me. As I looked at each and every one of them I began to cry. I realized that I had put every one of these girls in here and kept them locked up for so many years. I needed to ask for their forgiveness. What had I done? "The only thing you knew," came the soft but commanding voice, "All is not lost."

The realization of their faith and dependence upon me humbled me. I turned and guided them to the door that had once been only big enough for a mouse, then big enough for one person, but now big enough for a large crowd to exit. I still questioned how I was going to get them off of the ledge but much to my amazement as we stepped through the door, we were back in the main room, looking at the way out of the mountain. I looked at their faces, anticipating release from this prison, and their desire to leave this place was clear. They wanted out, to leave this place behind and never return again.

I started for the door but then stopped. The One Who Cares was not coming with us; he would stay behind,

Rescuing the Protector

but told us to leave this mountain of darkness. We all exited and watched his back to us, raising his arms, evoking the darkness to be gone and the light to remain. We felt a rush and surge of the gentlest, kindest and purest love that could ever be imagined. The mountain melted around him and was gone. The One Who Cares turned around and smiled at me, saying, "Well done." There was a look of complete satisfaction on his face as he gazed at us.

She is in a basement; the cement walls and floors are painted a stark white.

Chapter 14
Blood on a Cold Basement Floor

As Hope began to remember more details of the traumas she experienced, she saw images of herself in different scenes. As part of her fearless investigation, she agreed to record these memories. She wrote in the third person,

distancing herself from the memory, which made it easier to fully acknowledge the reality of that which she had endured.

~

January 2002

A young girl regains consciousness. She tries to move, and experiences a nauseating stab of pain. Her mouth has been taped and she begins to cry. She quickly realizes that if she continues to cry she will not be able to breathe. She tells herself to stop crying it will do no good. She tries to remember what happened and how she got here. She looks up at the only light in the basement. The light is on and the pull string is swaying with movement. Although there is no air current through the basement she dismisses the question. She is lying on the floor. She is alone and bound at the ankles; her wrists that are pulled behind her back are bound also. She is naked, beaten, cut and bleeding. She is in a basement; the cement walls and floors are painted a stark white. There is nothing in the basement, everything is shiny clean, and not a speck of dirt can be seen.

By the amount of dried blood on the floor she figures she has been here a while. She closes her eyes not believing that this has happened again! She tries to stop the images that now assault her mind. She begins to recall the images and memories of the previous encounter: Being stripped of her clothing, chased around the house with pepper spray, eyes burning, running into things, hearing the laughter of this spectacle. Then they catch her and surround her, each hit her and pushes her to the next until she stumbles and falls. They pick her up and take her to the bed. With handcuffs secure they throw knives at the ceiling above her on the bed. They wait for the knives to fall and place bets as to where the knives will enter her body. The young girl gets lucky; only one knife falls and goes into her left thigh. They argue as to who will get to remove it. The winner who claims the right to remove the knife pushes it in further then with a twist pulls it out slowly. They want the young woman to scream, but she remains silent and detached.

Roxie then yells at everyone to leave, she must be in a selfish mood. She strips off her clothes all the while humming a tune that is unfamiliar to the young woman but knows she will never forget it. Roxie picks her choice of toy for the evening and begins what she would call her lovemaking. To the young woman it is just another night of terror, pain, and torture. The young woman thinks at least tonight it is just Roxie.

Time For Healing

Somewhere between the singing and constant barrage of verbal abuse the young girl slips into unconsciousness. She awakens on the cement floor in the basement not knowing how long she had been there, what day it is, or even if it was light or dark outside. The pain rises in her as she lifts her head to look around. The effort takes most of all the strength that she has. Memories begin to seep into her mind now.

She was walking to a friend's house, a car pulls up along side her, and she begins to run. The car gives chase. Someone from inside the car leans out the window with a baseball bat and hits her behind the knees bringing her down immediately. She is writhing in pain on the side of the road; they gather her up and take her to this house. They drag her inside and make a game of removing her clothes. It is summer but they have a roaring fire going. Roxie brings a hot iron poker from the fire toward the young girl. She announces that this young woman belongs to her and thereby claims the right to "brand" her. She decides to burn the letter "R" on the young girl's left hand. The first burn sends and involuntary scream from the young girl as she struggles to make no sound but the pain is just too much. The stench of burned skin rises in the air. Some of the other women are getting sick and they run from the room to vomit. Roxie puts the iron in the fire again to re-heat it. One of the women whispers, trying to talk her out of finishing the brand. She tells Roxie that if she were to put a "R" on the young girl's hand there could be a possibility of it being linked to her. It would be better to not take that chance. Roxie concedes, so instead of finishing the "R" she just goes over again where she had previously burned to make it deeper. The smell is nauseating.

The young girl hears the voices ringing in her ears. Remembering those actions taken against her she tries to shut them out. She must not remember them, it is better to block them. She looks up at the pull string on the light; it is still swaying with movement. Why is it moving? The darkness returns.

~

It was quite a while before Hope was ready to revive this girl in the basement. There was more for her to see but she wasn't quite ready. She continued to gather her strength and realized that at the right time, she would be able to offer this girl the healing she needs.

If my heart were allowed to speak it would openly talk and admit my fears.

Chapter 15
Heart vs. Head

Hope began to realize the magnitude of this work, and that it would mean being willing to look at and accept every part of her difficult past. She became acutely aware of her own resistance.

Time For Healing

~

March 2002

For some reason I have such a struggle and feel real resistance inside of me when I try to speak. If my heart were allowed to speak it would openly talk and admit my fears, my needs and wants. I would not be afraid to ask to be held until I fell asleep.

But my head stops me saying, "Don't speak of such things, it will mean you are weak and that there is a place within you that can be hurt and wounded."

My heart wants to cry out for relief but my head silences me.

It is not that my heart wants to pour everything out; it just wants the choice, to share if the desire or need is there. My brain has told me for so long that these things should never be shared; I should never show emotion and never say I have any needs because it would be used against me.

If I had ever expressed my love for my friends, Roxie would become jealous and possibly take them away from me forever. It was always better to keep all those things to myself. No needs, no wants, no love, no comfort; that was just the way it was.

The ground is white in color, cracked with lines running out like a spider web ... I turn all around and I can see forever, but see nothing in sight.

Chapter 16
Desert Girl

Hope realized that she has, through the years, emotionally isolated herself from all feelings so as not to have to experience the pain of her past. She described the isolation by using graphic images of being abandoned in the desert and remembering more of the experiences that pushed her there for her survival. This started after Tammy was attacked and she couldn't forgive herself. Hope reached out to the isolated part of herself to offer healing.

~

May 2002
My dreams of the past few days were of a violent nature, in which once again I was fighting for my life physically, emotionally and spiritually. These dreams are so different this time, as they consist of color, emotion and slow motion visual details. I wake up two to three times a night, soaking wet with sweat, my body in a tight ball, huddled and shaking. My husband wakes me at one point and asks if I am okay. He said he thought I was crying. I do not recall why, only that it felt as though there were hundreds against only one... me. I would find myself battered, bruised, exhausted, and with only one thought and desire, to be left alone, isolated in this place where the earth is hard packed like baked pottery. The ground is white in color, cracked with lines running out like a spider web. Sometimes I stand or find myself sitting on the hot earth. I turn all around and I can see forever, but see nothing in sight. This place has no sound; it is devoid of color, only black and white. The only emotion that

is felt is one of complete, all encompassing isolation and aloneness. If I screamed no one would hear me. If I cried no one would see me. If I died no one would know. No one could know that was my plan. It is the only way I knew how to protect those that I loved. It was the only way I knew how to protect myself.

This girl of the desert stands alone, standing vigil over the essence of my life. I walk to her and she sees me in the distance, preparing for my arrival. I stop in front of her keeping a respectful distance between the two of us. Her eyes are dark and liquid. They hold so much sadness and isolation in them. I have never seen eyes like hers before; as she looks into my eyes I feel the isolation come in huge giant waves, and they crash into my heart, which rushes to my constricting throat. She has been waiting for me, gently calling me, but patient enough to wait until I was ready. This girl came to this desert right after the first time she was physically and sexually assaulted and almost killed.

When her friend Tammy was abducted, Desert Girl was restrained and forced to watch as they did the same things to Tammy that was done to her. I watched Desert Girl being held down, seeing the strain of her muscles as she fought to escape to rescue her childhood friend. Her veins were bulging, face red and her

Time For Healing

jaw and body rigid and tight. As she attempted to free herself, the skin on her wrist was being rubbed raw; her breath was silent until great gasps of air were sucked in. She was helpless and could not free herself; she could not help, she could only watch with the swirling motion of her head until it was done. This young girl, who was me, went to the desert and never left.

I took a step closer to this Desert Girl and she reciprocated with a step to me. I held out one arm and she responded by walking into my embrace. As I held her I could feel her body shake with tears, my own mingling with hers and we slid to the ground where I gathered her into the protection of my arms and rocked her. I invited a blessing from The One Who Cares. He anointed her head with oil and blessed her with comfort and a promise of release. We sat like this for a long time until slowly and gently changes started to occur.

The hot dry earth began to shift, and the air became full of moisture, until the desert was replaced by cool shallow seawater, the waves lapping gently on us, as if carrying away the isolation, the emptiness and the tears. Behind us the ground was like soft green peat moss, vivid colors and definition in the layout of the land. There were trees, flowers, bushes and a soft cool breeze that carried the songs of the birds in the air.

Desert Girl

The young girl of the desert was standing now looking around at this new place of safety, but there was still a heaviness and sadness about her. The thoughts and visions of memories still lived within her heart and mind. We needed to erect a monument of some sort to house those emotions, a place for remembrance and for storage, so they would no longer have to be carried. The plaque would say, "In Memory of Things Lost and of Things Gained." As Desert Girl placed the heavy load there for storage, she stood up and looked at me. A smile escaped her lips and my heart felt like it could fly. It was light, it was whole and I felt a relief of spirit, mind and body. She accepted the invitation to join me. As she joined my heart, my eyes could see, as though through eyes of an eagle. The sharpness, clarity, and distance were shocking.

As memories of the past flooded my mind's eye, I realized that I had always known the intent of others, whether evil or good. I had always chided myself for thinking that I was judging these people without knowing them. I did not realize that this was Desert Girl's endowment. It was one of her gifts to be used to protect me.

My world feels lighter, brighter and safer. At last, at last I can rest.

I see an image of a young woman ... in a hot air balloon. The balloon is tethered ... to a huge cement block.

Chapter 17
The Cement Block

As the process of looking and healing continued, Hope felt like it would never end. She felt she needed to run away from her life. She was dealing with the aspect of herself that felt restricted and chained to her experience.

Time For Healing

~

There is a quiet heavy sadness that I can't seem to break free of. It feels as though I will always feel this way. It is not like the sadness of two nights ago; this doesn't hurt, there's no physical pain.

I see an image of a young woman, 19 years old, in a hot air balloon. The balloon is tethered, keeping her at a certain altitude, unable to move in any direction. The line goes down to a huge cement block. This block is solid and around it stands seven women; the line is used to control her, to "keep her in line." These seven women are not her friends; they are the ones that attempt to control her. As I watch, I can see that this young girl, the Restricted Self, is actually holding on to the line with all her strength; she does not dare let go. I find myself in the balloon with her, and ask her to release the line, but she will not. I realize that the seven women are no longer standing there, but I see there is someone else by the cement block and realize it is The One Who Cares. I invite Him into the balloon with us. I place my hand over the heart of the Restricted Self and feel her isolation and sadness. I allow her to feel what is within my heart, my sadness and grief for her experience. The One Who Cares helps to connect us by placing His hands on

The Cement Block

both of our heads, and my head begins to tingle, with a sense of intense, burning warmth. It is an infusion of comfort and love and the young girl feels it too.

The One Who Cares returns to the cement block, removing the line, but continues to hold on. He beckons to the Restricted Self to let go of her end but still she resists. I place my hand over hers and encourage her, telling her it would be OK to let go. The One Who Cares suggests they do it together at the same time, and I hear the count: "One, two, three," and The One Who Cares and the Restricted Self release their hold simultaneously. Although it seems this should bring freedom, the cement block is still there and I know it must be destroyed, but not sure how. The One Who Cares takes out a small vial of sacred oil and pours it on top of the block. The oil keeps flowing until the top is covered, and the excess is running down the sides; the solid cement block begins to dissolve.

It was not a dramatic explosion or aggressive use of force that destroyed the block, the block is simply gone. The One Who Cares looks up and smiles. I am now floating free in the balloon, the young girl beside me. I actually feel movement, realizing that the sadness is gone and replaced with amazement and a quiet calm.

The pain feels like barbed wire has been forced down my throat, traversing throughout my body.

Chapter 18
Barbed Wire

Although she experiences a continuous flood of emotions, along with habitual instant reactions, Hope believed that things were subtly changing in her life. She desired healing and transformation, but was having a

Time For Healing

difficult time. She compared her feelings about going through this process to that of eating barbed wire.

∼

I do not want to be anywhere that I am. No matter where I go I am not comfortable. I am edgy, mildly agitated, out of sorts, restless and fidgety. There is no one word that truly expresses how I feel. I think I need to just keep myself busy and find things to do. Should I keep my mind off this feeling or is it something that I should explore? Is this something I need to confront and process? I don't know, but I need to go to my quiet place by the water.

I feel like I did two weeks after an assault, kind of cagey. I've tried to pin point my feelings; I feel alone, even though I know in my head I am not and this is a significant change from my past. Before this, I always thought I was on my own. I know I can envision the young women from the mountain. They helped the warrior; maybe they can help me.

I can see and feel the young women from the mountain surrounding, holding me up, and supporting me. They speak no words but I feel their calming affect. They do not help me process anything; they merely

Barbed Wire

help me understand that my choice to always being totally alone is no longer the way to live, and this is something I need to get used to. It is apparent to me at this point that I have already begun a process of change. There have been times recently when I have been by myself and find myself actually wanting company. Does this mean my barriers are weakening? I have so much conditioning to overcome!

I have so much to relearn, so much to change, it seems daunting. Sometimes I feel like I am pressuring myself to get through this quickly, before I am prepared and ready, and though it always turns out okay, it is so painful at times. The pain feels like barbed wire has been forced down my throat, traversing throughout my body, and then being yanked out at a horrific speed, tearing my guts apart. On days like these, I do not think I can endure the pain.

God help me please.

On the outskirts of my mind is a young woman whose hands are huge and grotesque, with claw like fingers ... a swampy like moss hanging from them.

Chapter 19
The Swamp Monster

Hope's guilt over her own role in what happened leads her to see a "monstrous" part of herself. She realized that she had hidden this part, not only from the rest of the world, but from herself, as well.

Time For Healing

~

On the outskirts of my mind is a young woman who, in her own mind, is so hideous, that she has hidden herself in a cave. This cave goes deep within the earth where no light can penetrate. She stands there waiting, watching and wanting to run, but is unable. Although she is young, her hands are huge and grotesque, with claw like fingers. There is a swampy like moss hanging from those hands, as if she is trying to hide or camouflage them. She is the Swamp Monster.

This is the young woman I cannot forgive, for her acts of violence and rage. It seems as though she has no heart; I will call her the Monstrous Self. I feel like she needs to see herself in a mirror and by doing so she will be so shocked and appalled that it will destroy her. I want her obliterated because she is very dangerous and a real threat. I know I need to look at her more closely, reach out and touch her, but she won't let me near her. She withdraws from me, thinking the evil within her will somehow transfer to anyone who touches her.

It takes a moment and then I realize that she is trying to protect me! Perhaps my first thoughts of her were wrong; maybe she does have some goodness in her. In her own

The Swamp Monster

way she has protected me by retaining the ugly and evil portion of my actions. I start to see her differently.

I invite The One Who Cares to meet her, but she withdraws from him as well. She does not feel worthy to be with him. He continues to tell her that he loves her, that she has purpose. He asks to take her hands, but she hides her ugliness. I tell her that she cannot pass the darkness or evil on to him for he is the one who created her. He gently asks again, and somehow she allows it, and he enfolds her into his arms, her back to his chest, and takes her hands into his. He sings to her and rocks her. He is singing a song from her childhood, "God So Loved the World." She relaxes in his embrace. I look at her hands, I cannot tell them apart from the hands of The One Who Cares.

I understand now that this young woman, who became the Monstrous Self, need not be destroyed, but there is something else we need to do; we have to look in the mirror together. I stand behind her and put my arms around her. I whisper in her ear, "It is OK now, I forgive you, thank you for protecting me." I had created her and I must now help her to see that she is not a sub-human creature. She has goodness, love and light within her. We stand before the mirror but she will not look up. I gently place my hands under her chin

Time For Healing

and pull her head upright so she can see her reflection. She sees that she is no longer a monster, but she is me, and we are one. She understands now that she truly has been forgiven, and as such, receives an invitation from The One Who Cares to go with him. He takes her hand and they leave the cave together.

I am standing now in the middle of the circle; I look at everyone in this circle and I feel the great power of their presence.

Chapter 20
Healing the Tortured One

It became clear why Hope was not been able to return to the girl on the basement floor. Together we realized that she must face everything this girl went through to free her. Hope was finally ready to attempt this.

Time For Healing

~

It's time to heal the young girl in the basement. I have been extremely hesitant and fearful of confronting this one. My body is the tightest it has ever been.

I have now remembered eight different times that I had been sexually assaulted. I know that there were more, but I have not been able to bring them to mind.

I am ready to begin:

In a basement is the young girl; she is bound at the ankles, her hands pulled behind her back. She has been gagged, cut, beaten, burned, bruised, and she is naked, lying on the floor. I sense the presence of both my Grandmother and The One Who Cares. I can see the young girl, this Tortured One, but I cannot see myself. I realize I am within the young girl and that I must separate from her.

Approaching her, she refuses to acknowledge me. She is resentful of me, I know nothing of her; I do not remember all that happened to her. The One Who Cares is standing behind me. He comes forward and bends down to speak with her. She looks up and past him

Healing the Tortured One

into my Grandmother's eyes. My Grandmother sends love and acceptance to this Tortured One, and feeling the compassion, she relaxes a bit. The One Who Cares leans down to this Tortured One and begins to loosen the duct tape from around her hands. He tells me that I must be the one to free her completely, but at this point she will not allow me near her. She will not accept my love or my sorrow or compassion for her. My heart feels as though it will break. She will never allow me to release her until I have seen what she wants me to see, that which she holds within.

I am told to speak aloud and describe everything I see. I panic at this thought, but decide to try. The young girl begins by showing me the torture that took place. I begin to speak in the first person, to truly accept that it was really me that this happened to. The events that took place are difficult to believe but I must acknowledge each one in order to heal this Tortured One.

My eyebrows are singed with a lighter, a flammable liquid poured on my abdomen and ignited, letting it burn until the blue is gone, then they throw a wet towel over it to extinguish it, then do it again.

I am in the dark, in a trunk of a car. They are taking me to the river. There are two trees close to each other.

Time For Healing

They strip me from the waist up and tie me between the trees. They shoot BBs at me, taking a step closer after each round. The ultimate goal is to get the BB to stick into my skin. They shoot at my back first then move to the front…that explains the small scars.

I am encouraged to continue to talk out loud as I remember these events. To this point I have complied, but I feel my body tighten as the next series of feelings and visions become clear. I can no longer speak, I go very deep and I detach. I do not hear anyone speaking or feel anyone nearby, but at the same time I know that I am not alone, so I venture forward. These things that I saw I am not sure that I will be able to share with anyone. Perhaps I could write them down as long as I tone them down…a lot.

Monkey bites in the shape of a "R" on my stomach
A clear plastic bag placed over my head to suffocate me
My face and body used for Roxie to sexually stimulate herself
Sex toys inserted into anal and vaginal orifices
Having oral sex performed on me for hours
My nipples sucked, rubbed and pinched until they would bleed
Hearing the same song hummed over and over
Having a gun held to my head, forcing me to say and

do things with the other women
The incessant verbal banter throughout the sexual abuse;
"I'm the only one that will and could love you now"
"You belong to me"
"You are my woman forever"
"Can you feel me baby?"
"You know that I could do this with someone else," and names all of my family and friends, "Maybe even your mom would enjoy this"
"Just tell me that you love me, come love me baby, love me"
"I chose you, I choose you now, marry me"
"I will never love anyone more than I love you and want you"

As the flood of these memories concludes, I feel my body in spasm. I am now ready to return to the basement and help the Tortured One. I approach her and she finally looks at me. She knows I have seen everything that happened to her. There are tears in her eyes as we cover her with a soft blanket and The One Who Cares anoints her head with oil. She receives this gift of care and I help her to stand, watching as the blanket falls and I see that her bonds are gone. I remove the tape from her mouth, a small sob escapes her lips and she collapses into my arms. I hold her and The One

Who Cares gathers us up as my Grandmother strokes the head of this Tortured One.

I understand now that I had to see and acknowledge everything that this Tortured One went through, every event, every thought and every feeling. By acknowledging and accepting all those things, I accepted her, all of her. That's what was important to her, that's the only way that she would come to me.

We walk outside the house, turn to look at the house, and then walk away from it toward a path that leads into a wooded area. We go to a safe place, a place of my childhood. It is a forested area where there is a small river with a waterfall. The surrounding area is very green, the ground soft as we step because of the lush, thick, cool moss. I feel the safety and security of this place.

I invite all the characters who have been healing to join us in a circle. The One Who Cares and I are joined by the Tortured One, the 14 year old and The Warrior from the mountain, my Grandmother, the isolated, Desert Girl and the Monstrous Self. The One Who Cares says a prayer for everyone in this circle and at this point I realize that my circle is not complete.

Healing the Tortured One

Although I had seen the Keeper of the Darkness nearby, I did not invite her into the circle, because she too seemed hesitant. But I realize now that she must be with us in our circle and she finally agrees.

The One Who Cares blesses her so that the pain in her compassionate heart will be eased and that she will find her path back to the light. His prayer continues and she is blessed that she will never again live in oppressive darkness and that the emotions she now feels will be ever flowing, never to be damned up again.

I am standing now in the middle of the circle; I look at everyone in this circle and I feel the great power of their presence. I feel a deep debt of gratitude, for without them I would have not survived, they kept me alive, they kept me sane and they kept me from becoming a monster.

I HATE this dream ... I am always being stalked by some kind of entity that can overtake me ...

Chapter 21
Dreams of Pain

It became more difficult for Hope to move through her memories with all the accompanying intense emotions and continue on in her daily life. She finally accepted the diagnosis of Post Traumatic Stress Disorder and agreed to a trial of medication in attempt to relieve her intense symptoms.

~

I was on the couch and I fell into a disturbing sleep. I saw, again, the many times and instances when I was assaulted. Every movement would cycle from slow motion to fast forward. I could feel the fear rise to my throat; my jaw is clenched tight, keeping any sound that might escape my lips silent. Then my recurring dream presents itself. My fear increases, I HATE this dream, I always feel that if I do not somehow wake myself that this dream could kill me. I am always being stalked by some kind of entity that can overtake me and cover me with the claustrophobic purpose of death.

I awakened suddenly, trying to calm myself down. I was slightly confused and unable to think clearly. I began to feel the fear rise, my body had tremors and my stomach was in distress. My gut felt like someone had taken a hot knife and stabbed me and was twisting it around. I sat down on a chair doubled over and started to cry. The pain was nauseating, the fear that I felt was accelerating and I was getting close to hysteria; every nerve in my body was on edge. I needed to calm myself down but my defenses were gone and I felt very vulner-

Dreams of Pain

able and helpless. For the first time in my life I could not help myself.

Lucky for me, I was in a place that I knew I was safe. I had come to my friends' home so many times before, seeking safety and always found it.

They talked to me about taking medication to assist me through this time, something that would help me fall asleep and stay asleep with no intrusive dreams; something that would calm my body spasms and reduce my startle reaction. This was not the first time they had discussed this with me. But I would not consider it, I hate taking medication especially anything long term.

I could feel the distress of everyone around me added to my own. I was fighting the pain, fighting the nausea, fighting the distress, fighting, fighting; it seems like all my life I have just been fighting and I could feel myself giving in. I just quit fighting and took in the pain, fear and distress and I decided at that point to take the recommended medication to help me through this. This was a big step for me.

I try to talk of my dream but it is so difficult. I feel like no one could really understand what this does to me. I'm in the process of connecting what happened to me in the past, to my reactions and behaviors today.

Time For Healing

Monday came and I stayed home from work. I felt so fragmented and so extremely tired. Every muscle in my body was screaming at me, every intake of air hurt. I wanted to curl up and be rocked and I wanted to sleep forever in quietness. I looked at myself in the mirror and saw nothing, no form, no life, no light, just dark empty space.

In the afternoon I was given the medication and instructions on how to take it. I wasn't happy about it but I admit now that there were no other options. I began taking them that night.

He pried the brick loose, pulling it out.

Chapter 22
The Brick Wall

I found myself wondering how Hope survived all these attacks and how she must have crept into her dorm room, unseen by roommates, after being assaulted. She could not remember and so attempted to see it.

~

I am asked to try to recall what I would do when I got home, after I was attacked and assaulted. I tried to remember, and visualize it, but a huge brick wall came slamming down right in front of me. The wall was as wide as my vision and as high. I took some steps backward from the wall; I didn't want to be near it and didn't want to touch it. The wall exuded a feeling of impenetrable power, a force that was tight, tenacious, confining and firm. There appeared to be no openings, loose bricks or any way to look at what was on the other side of the wall. Perhaps it was because I was not ready to see a way in.

I invited The One Who Cares to be there and help me look for a way to see through to the other side and realized there was a loose brick. I asked The One Who Cares to take the brick out and He pried the brick loose, pulling it out. He looked inside and he saw a young woman laying on a bed in the fetal position, holding herself, shaking in pain and rocking her body. I saw tears come down the face of The One Who Cares as He saw and felt the shock, loneliness, fear, embarrassment and torment in this young woman. He turned away and I looked through to see this Suffering

The Brick Wall

One. I looked upon her and I really saw her distress. She could not think clearly, she couldn't accept what really happened to her; maybe it was just a dream... how could this have happened to her? She just wanted to be left alone.

The next brick to be removed was slightly higher than the other. This view was one of the Suffering One in the shower; she was crying. The run off of water going down the drain was red. Her hair was matted with dried blood and bits of bone. The temperature of the water was as hot as she could possibly stand it. The water felt like knives slicing through her skin as it hit her open wounds and bruises, yet she would not get out of the shower; she stayed long after there was no more hot water. Shaking from the temperature of the cold water she continued to wash her body until the bar of soap was completely used up and there was no more. Watching her pick the bone pieces and wash the dried blood from her hair was almost more than I could bear. I felt sick. Then I remembered what had happened.

I could hear the bone shatter as I brought one of the women's forearm down across my thigh; I was trying to dislodge a knife from her hand. Bits of bone and blood spurted up into my face. I remember this image as I stood in that white porcelain shower, of the blood and a protruding bone coming out of the attacker's arm.

The next removal of a brick brought the sight of the young woman lying on the ground under some low hanging trees. She had been badly beaten and she was unconscious. When she came to, she did not know or recognize where she was and had no idea how to get home. She was confused and couldn't believe that this happened again.

Throughout this exercise I thought that I would experience anger, but this is something I never felt, everything except anger. This made no sense but I know it will. I looked at the wall it was almost all gone with only a few feet remaining. There was this quiet nagging sense that something hidden was still there, was it the key to my anger?

*I remember the enormous sadness of being alone...
of being totally alone.*

Chapter 23
Alone

Hope contemplated her isolation and admitted that it separated her from not only the people she loved, but also from her faith.

Time For Healing

~

Twenty-some years ago I felt that the only way to protect myself and those I loved was to isolate myself emotionally and sometimes even physically from everyone. This method allowed me to control my environment. It was easier on me emotionally to believe and feel that I was completely alone. If there were no one who could help me, I would have to be the one to protect myself and everyone else. People I cared about had been hurt physically and emotionally; I could and would prevent that from ever happening again!

There were times when I remember the enormous sadness of being alone, the feeling and the visual image of being totally alone. I am standing in the middle of the desert with no sound, color or motion; totally isolated I had no one to turn to. But that feeling would quickly pass. The thought of those that I cared about, possibly being brutally and savagely beaten, raped or having their personal property destroyed, would renew my resolve. I would repeat this thought to myself: "It is better to be alone. It is easier this way. It must be this way."

Because I had isolated myself from everyone, I guess I just figured that Christ was a part of that deal. I had done so much that would not be considered "Christ like" that I rejected any thoughts of help or forgiveness from Him.

I see myself standing half in shadow half in light.

Chapter 24
Shadows and Light

Anxiety came frequently to Hope and we talked about the feeling of waiting and watching from the shadows. She faced her fears and imagined herself speaking up to Roxie. Hope then moved on to the question of why no one stepped in to help her, and she began to feel anger for the very first time.

~

Tonight I have a feeling of uneasiness. I am slightly out of sorts, I feel like I am walking on eggshells. I see myself standing half in shadow half in light. As I separate the two and look at the part standing in the darkness I feel an apprehension, and a feeling of impending danger. I am standing against a wall. I look quickly around the corner realizing I am waiting for someone to pass. I realize I want nothing to do with whoever this person is, so I stay in the shadows and watch.

My anxiety is growing. I have an idea it is Roxie and my stomach tightens. I become nauseated. Doubts arise and I feel as though I am being thrown into a swirling confinement. I hear the words, "She can't hurt you anymore." I invite The One Who Cares to be there and to hold my hand. I put up some barriers so that Roxie cannot see me. With the shield in place I step out around the corner to face Roxie. She stops in her tracks. She cannot see me, but she can feel me. Roxie's appearance is older, with eyes that are barren and blank. There is no light in or behind her eyes. She has stopped about

Shadows and Light

ten feet in front of me. I feel a panic rise in me I want to turn and run from her. The phrase returns, "She can't hurt you anymore." I think I need to talk to her, so I drop my shield and Roxie sees me. I tell her that I release her; I will no longer play her sick games. I tell her to go away. I raise my right arm, palm facing her, and command her to leave. I look at her again and she is either getting smaller or I am getting bigger. My body is tingling and I feel like I am floating. This sensation is alarming, but I also feel a great sense of relief.

I turn and continue up a sidewalk. It takes me to the house that my parents lived in when I went to college. I stand in front of their house. It is empty. I wonder where my family is. I am disappointed that they are not there. I wanted them to be there. I wanted them to just step in regardless of my answers to them that all was well. I didn't want to have to ask for help. If I had asked, and something happened to them, I don't think I could have forgiven myself. If they had just stepped in without my consent I think I would have allowed it. But they did not. They accepted my insistence that everything was okay. I said I was just under a lot of stress from college life.

Why didn't my parents step in? They asked me several times if I was okay, that they felt something was not right. Each time, I insisted that I was fine, and they would back away. I remember my parents even coming to see me for a surprise visit and took me out to dinner. Their questions were passively inquisitive. I negated their concerns with ease. Why didn't they inquire further?

So here at their house I keep asking the questions, "Why is this house empty? Did they talk to anyone about their concerns? Why didn't they do anything? Where the hell are they?"

The only thing I can think of is that my parents never experienced pure evil, and so how could they recognize the extent of the danger I was in?

Tammy was dead; she committed suicide 15 years ago.

Chapter 25
Tammy

I had asked Hope several times if she knew the whereabouts of Tammy, her childhood friend who was assaulted as retaliation against her. Eleven months after the telling she found the courage to investigate. She

found the worst possible answer, but it firmed her resolve and changed the course of history.

~

September 2002
So, another sucker-punch. I called a friend from grade school to ask if she knew where Tammy was and she told me that Tammy was dead; she committed suicide 15 years ago.

I feel a sense of deep sadness, responsibility and guilt, anger and grief.

My emotions are cycling at a furious pace. There are times when the anger rises up in me so rapidly and in such an explosive way that I want to scream at anyone just because they are breathing! I am breathing, Roxie is breathing and Tammy is not! I feel like getting up and walking away never to return. How do I deal with these feelings? I feel absolutely responsible for Tammy's death; if she had not known me, she might still be alive! I grieve for a friend who died because of retaliation against me. I must act and it must be now.

My plan is to keep Roxie off the streets. I made a list of what I must do:

Write a notarized letter to the State's Attorney
Find out more information regarding the status of her case
Tell the six other women of Tammy's death
Ask them to write letters
Tell them I'm going to name them
Express my anger toward them
Find Tammy's Mom; tell her I just heard about her death
Back off and look at the big picture (make sure I'm doing this for the right reasons; just to make Roxie suffer is not good enough)
Be ready to accept the consequences of these actions

I am afraid to step fully into the light and have all of me seen.

Chapter 26
Resolution

I asked Hope what resolution would mean to her. I wondered how she would come to the point of peace and eventual acceptance about these events.

Time For Healing

~

What does resolution mean to me emotionally?
A sense of wholeness
Space
The heaviness lifted
Stillness and quiet
Oneness
Color
Light

How do I find resolution from here?
Give myself permission to set the weight down
Step into the light
Ask for help out of the shadows
More forgiveness
Let the grief go

So here I am feeling very scrambled. I did write the letter to Roxie's Psychiatrist and a whirlwind of action has happened because of it. I have named all the people involved and I am now in a mild state of shock in that the prison Psychologist has contacted the District Attorney's Office and they are gathering evidence, including medical records, interviews and statements from the six women, all for the purpose of prosecuting Roxie.

Resolution

I am afraid. I am afraid to put down this heavy burden. I am afraid to step fully into the light and have all of me seen.

What if she is found not guilty?

I would like to break this link as soon as possible.

Chapter 27
Unresolved Connections

Six months after the letters were sent to the State District Attorney's office, Roxie was in prison, the correspondence firming up the case against her by the state. She had been charged with multiple assaults, carrying concealed weapons and other crimes over the years. The letters served as a history of the intensity of Roxie's deranged mind and unfathomable actions.

In some cases a continued psychic connection exists between victims and their abusers. It certainly existed between Hope and Roxie and it was because of this connection that Roxie was extradited to another state where she would be tried for murder and eventually kill herself.

One Sunday morning, Hope woke up feeling anxious and uneasy; she knew that it had something to do with Roxie. She called the prison to inquire but didn't learn what happened for several days. What she read overwhelmed us both.

~

So last Sunday morning after I woke up, I felt that there was a "disturbance in the force." I felt like I did 20 years ago, full of fear, dread, and anxiety. I knew something was not right! I felt sick, my nerves were in hyper mode and I couldn't sit still. I was watching everyone, looking to see if anyone was following me.

I called the office of the psychologist who was in charge of Roxie at the prison and left a message, telling her I

Unresolved Connections

felt like something was wrong. At that point all I could do was wait. Monday came and I hadn't heard anything, so I called again. I was told that there had been an incident on Sunday with Roxie. The incident would be explained to me in a letter and it would be faxed to me while I was on the phone with the psychologist. There was no other explanation, so I was left to my imagination and total uneasiness.

I found an office that had a phone and a fax machine. I received the fax and read it. I was overwhelmed and totally unnerved. I still had a connection with Roxie. I can't even begin to describe how this feels, invaded, like my mind or my thoughts are not my own. I can't believe we are still connected! Will I ever be free of this woman? I talked with the doctor for about 45 minutes, and she believes that this connection can be dissolved. I really hope she is right. I would like to break this link as soon and as fast as possible. I know and understand that I may still have emotional reactions, and I can deal with that, I just don't want this paralyzing power of connection. Phantoms and memories are one thing, but what I have just gone through is too much. I want it out, gone, ejected, stripped, dismantled, eradicated, dissolved, defeated, excised, and banished!

Our hope and prayers are that you will have peace, and that you will be able to find release and freedom.

Chapter 28
The Letter

Dear Hope,
Let me begin by saying how sorry I am about what you have gone through and have had to endure all these years. I have been reviewing all my sessions and all my

personal notes on Roxie and only now do I realize that I did not fully understand the FULL measure and the immensity of her behavior and capabilities.

It is a true travesty of injustice. No person or persons should have been allowed to experience what was done to you. I can only imagine the horrific affect this has had on you and in your life.

Early Sunday morning, the guards responded to Roxie's room where they discovered her as they called it, "acting in a bizarre behavior." They called in the Floor Supervisor who immediately started the remote observation camera and recorded what she was doing.

I can't even begin to describe her behavior and language nor do I wish to. Watching that video made me sick to my stomach. I have worked in this field for many years and I have NEVER been so affected by a patient. I thought that I had heard it all before, maybe the difference now is that I have a visual. I have to admit that when I was back in the safe confines of my office I wept for you. I don't think that I need to tell you specifically what she was doing and what she said because you have already lived through it. I do feel however that I need to explain to you why you felt such a disturbance Sunday morning so much so, that

The Letter

you left that message on my phone. After viewing the video, then listening to your message I was not surprised that you called.

You still have a connection with her, and she with you. This happens in many cases of traumatic events. You may wish not to think this or may think that it is absurd, how and why you would want to keep a connection. You may say, "I want nothing to do with this individual or experience, so why would I hang onto it?" It is not on a conscious level that this connection exists. In all probability you fine-tuned this connection as a survival technique, using pure instinct as a way to protect and defend. Let me assure you that just as you developed this connection you can also dissolve this connection. I would highly recommend that you enlist the help of an individual that can take you through this process. Release this unconscious tie that continues to bond the two of you together, otherwise this may, and probably will happen again.

If you were my patient I would say by what I know of you that a diagnosis of Post-Traumatic Stress Disorder (PTSD) would be plausible and you could receive some type of care and attention (i.e., medication, counseling) to help alleviate any of the varying symptoms produced by such a traumatizing occurrence. I

Time For Healing

hope that you have received or are in the process of receiving some type of assistance, if not, PLEASE consider this avenue as a means to help you release and progress forward.

Monday afternoon, all parties met with the Judge to watch the video and I can safely say that not one person was unaffected by what they saw. We had to stop the video several times to allow individuals to recompose themselves, including the judge. When the video had ended there was such a deafening silence in the courtroom, no one could move. We were paralyzed with fear, nausea and utter disbelief. When the Judge could finally speak, he asked my opinion if this was a reenactment of some sort or an attempt at subterfuge. I said; let us ask the six witnesses for the prosecution. The Judge turned to question each one individually. Their response was monumental; they were all in hysterical grips of crying. One answered first, that it was indeed something that had happened and gave the date and where it had occurred and then she vomited; the others in turn followed suit. After a recess, council and I were called back into chambers with the Judge. I affirmed vehemently that from my sessions with and knowledge of Roxie this was definitely a reenactment of a past encounter with you. The Judge responded that in light of this new information, it was in the best interest of all involved to extradite Roxie to [state name withheld]

The Letter

to be held there until she is tried for the alleged murders of two nineteen year old teenagers. Upon completion of the trial and sentencing there, she will in fact be tried in this state for the alleged crimes stated on the dockets of the court. They are preparing the extradition papers today, (Monday). If all goes as planned she will be flown to (state name withheld) under heavy sedation and guard on Saturday, (date withheld.) On my way out of the Judges Chambers the Judge stopped me and asked me to tell you thank you for what you have done.

From what I was told by the DA the case against Roxie in (state name withheld) is very strong. They have witnesses and a DNA match. The DA here has told the prosecution in (state name withheld) they would assist in any type of information sharing that would be allowed.

Hope, my heart is in pain to the point that I may need to seek some medical relief and counseling myself. I tell you this not to add any guilt or weight on you, but to let you know that there are those who have been touched by your story and have been awakened to the acknowledgment of evil. There are people who wish to champion for your cause because of your strength and courage to follow your sense of right and wrong and to live your code of values every day of your life. This woman has harmed so many people for so many years

Time For Healing

it is time, time for it to end, time for evil to be extricated out of this society. It does not belong here.

Our hope and prayers from all of us here are that you will be well; that you will have peace, and that you will be able to find release and freedom. You are indeed a remarkable human being.

With Affection and Respect,

Dr.'s name withheld.

I am safe. This is the beginning.

Chapter 29
Then vs. Now

Two years have passed since we began this process of healing and I asked Hope to tell me how she has changed and how her life is different.

Time For Healing

~

Looking at the changes that have happened within me, I can see how far I have come.

In the past it was shadows, shadows, the shadows chasing me. A constant frequency of a straight line; there was never any deviation, no up, no down, nothing to the right, nothing to the left, no rhythm, no flow, flat… straight.

When I would glance at a sunset I saw only two colors; yellow and orange and that was only if I allowed myself to be still for that moment, otherwise my world was gray.

Then came my journey into healing. I slowly began to realize that the shadows were not chasing me; I was running from them, so I stopped. I looked into those shadows, into their eyes, and to my amazement I saw my own lifeless eyes.

So how does one find hope and healing? By simply having the desire to be whole and to heal the wounded, bleeding heart. This is the beginning.

Then vs. Now

My desire was to tell my story and from there, a burden of years and years of holding and hiding came to an end. In its place I found love, anger, sadness, guilt, peace, remorse, grief, joy, happiness, color and life! I found life! For the first time in a long time I was able to feel my life, smell it, touch it, taste it and hear it in all its wondrous breathtaking power. I could breathe again!

My days and nights are now filled with color, light, love and hope. I am safe. This is the beginning. So Be It.

My story has been told and light has illuminated the deepest, darkest corners of my soul.

Epilogue

And now the narrative comes to a close. The story is done: a perpetrator is dead and this victim is finally free. She has reclaimed her life and her strength has made this possible. She had the courage to look at her past and confront, accept, forgive and heal every part of herself. This transformation is possible for everyone, no matter what the details of their trauma, if they are willing to risk stepping from their safety zone into the unknown.

∼

So how does this story end? The simple answer is it doesn't. My story, my life goes on, it changes everyday. Each sunrise is a new day with love to be given and received, emotions to be felt and processed, goals to be made and achieved, lessons to be learned and mistakes to be corrected. I am grateful that my story does not end here, because I realize that all that has happened to me, all that was done to me, has had a great effect, but it is not the most important part of me.

Am I completely purged of the shadows? Do I have this euphoric feeling, "all better now," like it never happened? No. What happened to me was horrifying, de-basing, and so shockingly disturbing that sometimes I still have nightmares and awake in cold sweats. Sights, sounds and smells can still evoke a memory, only now I don't shut down or become paralyzed with fear. Those old methods of self-preservation, like isolation, silence or constant movement rarely bring me comfort or make me feel safe now. Instead

Epilogue

I feel the silence is deafening, the isolation is agonizing and the constant movement just wastes my energy.

My story has been told and light has illuminated the deepest, darkest corners of my soul. I continue to look, feel, observe and grieve, until understanding pierces my heart and mind, and I realize I am free. I am free to choose my reactions. I am free to define who I am, free to be loved and to love. I choose to be free.

~

Authors Note:
The statistics regarding Post-Traumatic Stress Disorder are astounding, with millions of people experiencing these profound symptoms every day. Despite the availability of therapeutic modalities, many PTSD sufferers choose not to seek treatment for a variety of reasons. Shame, guilt, fear of disclosure and the stigma of mental illness lock victims into a lifetime of hell and despair. My hope is that this story, now told, will lead others to find wholeness, healing and finally, freedom.

PTSD Information and Resources

What is PTSD?
Post-Traumatic Stress Disorder is a psychological disorder affecting individuals who have experienced or witnessed profoundly traumatic events, such as torture, murder, rape or wartime combat. This disorder is characterized by recurrent flashbacks of the traumatic event, nightmares, irritability, anxiety, fatigue, forgetfulness and social withdrawal.

A traumatic event is defined as one in which the person experienced or witnessed an event that "involved actual or threatened death or serious injury, or a threat to the physical integrity of self or others and which involved intense fear, helplessness or horror."

The emotional effects of trauma can include:
- Recurrent terror and rage
- Shifting emotions between intensity of feelings and numbness
- Immeasurable sorrow and deep grief
- Shattered dreams
- Intrusive memories
- Flashbacks
- Freezing with fright
- Fear of insanity
- Guilt, shame, helplessness, loneliness, alienation

Statistics:

The 2006 National Institute of Mental Health Report states that approximately 7.7 million American adults, age 18 and older, or about 3.5 percent of people in this age group in a given year, are diagnosed with PTSD.

Community-based studies have revealed a lifetime prevalence for Post-Traumatic Stress Disorder ranging from 1% to 14%. Studies of at-risk individuals (e.g., combat veterans, victims of natural disasters or criminal violence) have yielded prevalence rates ranging from 3% to 58%.

Approximately 30% of those who have spent time in war zones experience Post-Traumatic Stress Disorder.

PTSD can develop at any age, including childhood, but research shows that the median age of onset is 23 years old.

The prevalence of Post-Traumatic Stress Disorder in women is twice that of men.

Women who are victims of crime, and torture and concentration camp survivors suffer the highest rates of Post-Traumatic Stress Disorder

Symptoms of PTSD:

According to the American Psychiatric Association, Post-Traumatic Stress Disorder can be seen as an overwhelming of the body's normal psychological defenses against stress. Thus, after the trauma, there is abnormal function of the normal defense systems, which results in certain symptoms. The symptoms manifest themselves in three different ways:
1. Re-experiencing the trauma
2. Persistent avoidance
3. Increased arousal

First, the individual may have distressing recollections of the trauma, and may re-live the experience as terrible dreams, nightmares or as daytime flashbacks of the event. External cues in the environment may remind the person of the event and as a result, the psychological distress of the exposure to trauma is reactivated, or brought back, by internal thoughts or memories. Persons also can experience physical reactions to stress, such as sweating and rapid heart rate. The post-traumatic symptoms can be identical to those symptoms experienced when the actual trauma was occurring.

The second way that symptoms manifest themselves is by persistent avoidance. The avoidance refers to the person's efforts to avoid trauma-related thoughts, feelings, activities or situations that may trigger memories of the trauma. For example, a person may develop decreased interest in activities that used to give pleasure, detachment from other people, restricted range of feelings, and sadness that lead to the fear of a limited future.

The third symptom is described as an increased state of arousal, which manifests itself as sleep disturbances, irritability, outbursts of anger, difficulty concentrating, increased vigilance, and an exaggerated startle response when shocked or surprised

Treatment and Resources:

The use of Selective Serotonin Reuptake Inhibitors (SSRIs) has been studied at length and proven useful in decreasing and resolving the continued effects of PTSD. The combination use of medications, such as Paxil, Zoloft, Lexapro or Prozac, along with psychological counseling, whether traditional cognitive behavioral therapies, guided imagery or alternative methods, seem to have a more profound effect than when used singularly.

There are many reputable resources available for increased understanding of PTSD. There are websites, books, articles and support groups sponsored by local and national organizations.

The following websites are useful for gathering more information regarding PTSD.

The National Center for Post-Traumatic Stress Disorder
http://www.ncptsd.org
This website contains fact pages on PTSD itself as well as pages specifically about sexual assault

http://www.ncptsd.org/facts/specific/fs_female_sex_assault.html (Sexual assault of women) http://www.ncptsd.org/facts/specific/fs_male_sexual_assault.html (Sexual assault of men)

http://www.ptsdinfo.org
This is a campaign to inform the public about the emotional injury of Post-Traumatic Stress Disorder

National Institute of Mental Health
1-866-615-NIMH(6464)
http://www.nimh.nih.gov
This site includes fact sheets, resources, and articles.

American Psychological Association
http://www.apa.org/topics/topicptsd.html

This site lists articles, books and videos on trauma and other psychological disorders

National Mental Health Association
1-800-969-NMHA(6642)
http://www.nmha.org
Easy to read information with many resources including support groups as well as their
Crisis Line 1-800-273-TALK

Health Journeys
http://www.healthjourneys.com
This website sells Guided Imagery CDs and books on PTSD, relaxation techniques, as well as research findings regarding the success in utilizing these techniques for individual healing.

Delphi University
http://www.delphiu.com
Delphi University is the birthplace of RoHun™ Therapy and is an International School of Alternative, Complementary Healing and Transpersonal Psychology.

EMDR/ Eye Movement Desensitization and Reprocessing
http://www.emdr.com
"Strongly recommended" by The American Psychiatric Association as another form of treatment for PTSD

About the Author:

Amy Groger Martin is a Doctor of RoHun™, Transpersonal Psychotherapy, and a Board Certified Nurse Practitioner with three decades of clinical experience. Her private practice, Healing Therapies, is located in Niantic, Connecticut, where she offers unique and dynamic transformational opportunities to both individuals and groups. She writes a syndicated monthly column called "Time for Healing," which appears in the newspapers of Southeastern Connecticut and Rhode Island.

In addition to her writing and healing practice, Amy loves music, playing and writing for harp, piano, flute and guitar, creating songs to uplift the spirit and soothe the heart.

She, her husband and two daughters have enjoyed living all over the United States and New South Wales, Australia, gathering a circle of dear friends around the world.

For information about RoHun™ Therapy, the purchase of this book, inspirational art and music, go to her web site: www.Time4Healing.com.

Be sure to visit www.time4healing.com for a free monthly newsletter, updated articles and a brand new Emotional Self Assessment Tool. This insightful, thought provoking exercise will help clarify your thoughts and emotions, and get you started on your path toward lasting transformation.